Black and Neurodi

"The intersectionality of being Black and Neurodiverse".

By: Oluseyitan Ojedokun

Insight into the life of a Neurodiverse Black girl from the Midlands, as she embarks on her journey through the UK school system.

This book unveils and highlights the unique experiences of neurodiverse people of colour and the many challenges they face.

In this book, 24-year-old, British-Nigerian, Oluseyitan Ojedokun gives an account of her **struggles** through school. She shares the many dreams and goals she had, despite the feeling of constant dismay.

Table of Contents

Cultural Differences 6

I hate School 17

Late Diagnosis 42

Light at the end of the Tunnel 49

My Diagnosis 57

Lack of funding 68

My Superpower 74

Synopsis

My name is Oluseyitan Ojedokun. Oluseyitan is a Yoruba name that means "God has done it". My name in the past has often been mistaken as many things, such as "Shy-eat-her, "Shay-tar", oh and how can I forget "Olu-Say-it-an". My name is neither and is pronounced O-lou-shay-ee- t-oah.

With the anxiety that came every time my name was read out by a supply teacher on the register, and the many failed and forgotten attempts that came after meeting people for the first time, I concluded that "Shey" would be my alias.

Despite being summoned to the yellow table at the tender age of 6 and taken out of the classroom for "special" lessons at 7. It was not until 16, when I failed 7 out of 9 GCSEs, that it was made apparent that there was something deeper going on.

I wish I could say that I didn't try. I wish I could say that I didn't have years and years of private tuition. I wish I could say that I didn't pray. Regardless of all these things, I still failed.

It wasn't until "year 11+" and my second unsuccessful attempt to attain my GCSE Maths and English that suspicions were raised. It was then that the possibility of Dyslexia was a thought. However, at this point, I had not been tested nor screened. It was not until University that I was given the opportunity to explore this further. It was then that I was diagnosed by an Educational Psychologist. Not only did I have Dyslexia, but Dyspraxia and Dyscalculia too.

I sit down today, and I write this book in utter disbelief and amazement. I once believed that I would never amount to much. At the time of writing this book, I am 24 years old, a BA (Hons) Graduate and a MA Graduate with Distinction.

I attribute these accomplishments to my name; God has done it. Truly it has been a miracle to get to where I am today.

I hope that my story will encourage people, those who are neurodiverse and those who are not. If you are reading this and you suspect that you or someone close to you may be neurodiverse, I hope that my story will inspire you to advocate to get screened and tested as soon as possible. Earlier screening and diagnosis would have allowed me the opportunity to access the support and the tools I needed to help me navigate school better.

Before I continue, I think it would be useful to provide some definitions for my diagnoses:

Dyspraxia - a common disorder that affects movement and coordination. Dyspraxia does not affect your intelligence. It can affect your coordination skills - such as tasks requiring balance, playing sports, or learning to drive a car.

Dyslexia - a common learning difficulty that mainly causes problems with reading, writing, and spelling. It's a specific learning difficulty, which means it causes problems with certain abilities used for learning, such as reading and writing. Intelligence isn't affected.

Dyscalculia - a specific and persistent difficulty in understanding numbers which can lead to a diverse range of difficulties with mathematics.

Additionally, within this book, the link between race and Neurodiversity has also been explored. Through conducting research and sharing findings, going forward I hope to better inform teaching practices.

Black and Neurodiverse

Oluseyitan Ojedokun

1

Cultural Differences
Growing up in a Nigerian Household

Academic excellence is highly valued in Nigerian households across all classes, as education is seen as a pathway out of poverty and a means of achieving success. From a young age, children are taught to respect education and to strive for excellence in their studies. This was certainly the case in my upbringing, despite coming from a lower to middle-class Nigerian household.

My parents, like many other Nigerians, had a strong emphasis on education, and it was deeply ingrained in our family's legacy. My mother holds a master's degree, and my father a PhD. Their pursuit of academia and academic excellence set the path straight for me and my sister.

We were encouraged to work hard and strive for success, particularly in our studies.

However, the pressure to excel academically was not the only thing that was valued in my household. My parents also placed a strong emphasis on character and integrity, and they instilled in us a strong work ethic and a commitment to excellence in all aspects of our lives. They encouraged us to pursue our passions and to be well-rounded individuals who could contribute positively to society.

While academic success was highly valued in my household, it also came with a great deal of pressure. The expectations were sky-high, and anything less than excellence was often considered a failure. I felt this pressure keenly, and it was compounded by the fact that many of my relatives were successful doctors, lawyers, and high-standing professionals. My Grandfather, Olasupo Ojedokun, was the second Director-General of the Nigerian Institute of International Affairs, and his career in academia inspired me. In the 1960s, he received numerous scholarships to study in the USA and UK. He accepted a scholarship from the Commonwealth to study at the London School of Economics and came over-with his lovely wife, who then gave birth to three children, including twins one of which is-my Father.

Despite the high expectations, I found myself struggling to meet them. Although I worked hard, I often felt that I was not achieving the same level of success as my peers. It was not until later in life that I came to understand that this was likely due to neurodiversity. While I was never formally diagnosed at the time, looking back, I can see that I likely had undiagnosed learning disabilities that made academic success even more challenging for me.

As a child, even though I struggled with academics, my family legacy gave me hope that I too could achieve greatness. Despite facing the roadblocks of being a Black person navigating academia, and professional lives with Nigerian accents, it encouraged me. Their hope and determination helped me to persevere and remain optimistic about my future, despite not receiving much support and encouragement from teachers through the years.

In Nigerian households, academic excellence is highly valued as it is seen as a pathway out of poverty and a means of achieving success. The pressure to excel academically can be overwhelming, but it is important to remember that success can take many different forms. Pursuing one's passions and finding fulfilment in one's career, as well as making a positive impact in one's community, are also measures of success. By emphasising the importance of character, integrity, and a commitment to making a positive impact in the world, parents can help their children find success and fulfilment in their own unique ways, regardless of any challenges or limitations they may face.

Growing up with Carers

With Parents working full-time jobs, Nursery, childminders and summer school were a big part of my sisters and my life. A lot of my favourite memories as a child were in these places. I have a loving memory of the foods that we used to eat, from Banana and Custard at Nursery to Pounded Yam rolled up in miniature balls with Okra stew and Beef at home. I remember the chunky cutlery, the bright colours and the different animal patterns at Nursery.

There was always a huge focus on creativity and opportunities to create. I remember Nursery being an artsy place, I still have all my first art pieces in a file, from paper Mache's to paintings and drawings. I loved my nursery, they first introduced me to my creative side. At this point, I had not been diagnosed, however, even my father recalls, my remarkable observation skills and a passion for picking out my own clothes at the tender age of 2.

There was a close relationship between my parents and the Nursery, the staff were not diverse, however, there was an understanding of my Nigerian background. The nursery was independent and family-run, and my parents were fond of the lady in charge, "Paula". The Nursery were in constant communication with my parents, sharing updates on my progress, unlike my primary school, where my parents were often left in the dark about my progress.

Growing up with a Lack of Diversity

I attended a Catholic primary school located in the Midlands. It was an area predominantly inhabited by white people, which meant that for a long time, my sister and I were some of the few Black children. To make matters worse, I had undiagnosed neurodiverse conditions at the time, which made it harder for me to fit in. The lack of diversity in the school only added to the difficulties I faced, and I found myself hating school. Although I couldn't pinpoint the reasons for my negative school experience as a young child, I knew that I stood out like a sore thumb, and it was uncomfortable.

Throughout my time in school, I found that teachers had a higher level of prejudice than students. Incidents were often subtle, yet deliberate. I remember one day, a sock was intentionally thrown by a teacher and hit me in the face. It was a hurtful act, but it was quickly dismissed as a harmless joke. I wrote a letter to report the incident, hoping that something would be done about it. But unfortunately, nothing happened. I remember feeling frustrated and unable to express this, a common theme and feeling that would acquaint me going forward.

As a family, we often revisit the instance where a teacher rebutted that my sister should not attend university, but should however pursue a career in athletics, "something a bit more suited to her skillset". We laugh today, because not only did she attend university, but she is now a Qualified

Paediatric Social worker. We both faced a lot of ignorance throughout school.

We can reflect on this incident, considering the impact of assumptions and unconscious bias, and how it can affect the opportunities and experiences of individuals. We also recognise the importance of overcoming such biases, allowing us to explore other opportunities behind these ill-informed expectations.

The lack of diversity I faced did not stop at school. Notwithstanding my parents' efforts to enrol me into a predominantly Caribbean supplementary school, attend a monthly Nigerian Fellowship and take me on trips to the motherland. Sunday to Sunday, I found myself in a predominantly White majority Church.

As I grew older, I began to gain a better understanding of the systemic issues that contributed to the lack of diversity around me. I learned about the socioeconomic factors that perpetuated inequality and limited access to opportunities for people of colour. Through this understanding, I became more intentional about seeking out spaces that were diverse and inclusive. Being a part of these diverse communities has been a transformative experience for me. I have been able to learn from people with different backgrounds and experiences, and I have been exposed to new perspectives and ideas that have expanded my own worldview.

Disability and Neurodiversity in Black Communities

In addition to highlighting the importance of these conversations for the Black British Diaspora, it is also vital to promote awareness and acceptance of disabilities in countries such as Nigeria and like it, where the stigma attached to these conditions creates a significant barrier for individuals to seek help and support.

The World Disability report estimates that over 25 million people in Nigeria are living with disabilities. Despite this staggering number, the mere mention of disability and neurodiversity is often met with hesitancy and considered a taboo topic. In a society where disability is viewed as a curse or path of misfortune, conversations and testing are avoided, leaving individuals to navigate their challenges alone. By amplifying the voices of those who may not have a platform to be heard, we can work towards creating a more inclusive and supportive society.

My aspiration is for you, the reader, to gain a deeper understanding of some of the challenges faced through comprehending my perspectives.

I am an individual who happens to be neurodiverse, embedded in multifaceted cultures, resulting in multifaceted experiences. I am a testament that intersectionality can be a beautiful thing, creating a unique identity that cannot be defined by any one factor.

This can be accounted for in the term 'Black,' which encompasses Africans, Caribbeans, parts of the Latinx community, African American people, and more. In addition to the term 'Neurodiverse' that covers a spectrum of conditions. From Autism to ADHD, Dyslexia, Dyspraxia, Dyscalculia and so many more.

For me both my race and neurodiversity have vastly contributed to shaping my outlook on life.

2

I hate School

A skewed history for many Black British children and UK Educational Institutions

In 1960s and 1970s numerous Black British children were wrongly identified as "educationally subnormal" and subsequently placed in ESN Schools. Schools for pupils deemed to have a "low intelligence". Attending an ESN school was a one-way ticket to a life of low-paying manual labor. The label was paralysing, killing any hope for self-confidence or ambition. Sadly, black students were more likely to be sent to these schools, as revealed by a leaked report from the Inner London Education Authority in 1967. The report found that twice as many black immigrant children attended ESN schools compared to mainstream schools.

The injustice of this system was compounded by the fact that it was based on flawed, biased testing methods. The IQ tests used to determine "educational sub-normality" were designed by and for white, middle-class children, with little consideration given to the diverse cultural and linguistic backgrounds of Black children. This resulted in Black children being unfairly penalised for their differences, rather than being supported in their individual needs and strengths.

Even more insidious was the prevalence of racist ideology among some educators and administrators, who actively sought to perpetuate the marginalization of Black children. The 1969 report by headteacher Alfred Doulton, claiming that West Indian children had lower IQs, was just one example of this pseudoscientific racism. Such attitudes contributed to a wider culture of prejudice and neglect, in which Black children were seen as lesser and their potential was systematically stifled.

But it wasn't just the ESN schools that were failing Black children. The curriculum itself was often devoid of Black history and culture, perpetuating a myth of white superiority and Black inferiority. Black children were rarely taught about their own heritage, and the achievements of Black people were largely ignored. This lack of representation and recognition had a detrimental effect on the self-esteem and self-worth of Black children, who were left feeling invisible and unimportant.

The consequences of these failures continue to reverberate today, and a skewed history cannot be forsaken. Black children are still underrepresented in higher education and are more likely to experience discrimination and exclusion within schools. The ongoing disparities in educational attainment and opportunities between Black and white children are a testament to the enduring legacy of these failures.

A long and complicated history for Neurodiverse Students

The UK schooling system has a long and complicated history, and its treatment of neurodiverse students is no exception. Neurodiversity is a term used to describe the range of neurological differences that exist in the human population. This includes conditions such as autism, ADHD, dyslexia, and others. Neurodiverse students face a number of challenges in the UK education system, which has historically struggled to accommodate their needs.

The history of the UK schooling system's treatment of neurodiverse students can be traced back to the late 19th century. In 1883, the Royal Commission on the Blind, the Deaf, and Dumb was established to investigate the education and welfare of disabled children in the UK. The commission's findings led to the establishment of special schools for blind, deaf, and mute children. This was the first step in the segregation of disabled students in the UK education system.

In the UK, schools have long been touted as institutions that are supposed to help students develop their full potential. However, this has not always been the case, especially for students who are neurodiverse. Over the years, the UK schooling system has failed to accommodate neurodiverse students, leading to significant difficulties for these students and their families.

The term "neurodiversity" refers to the idea that neurological differences should be recognised and respected as a natural part of human diversity. This includes conditions such as autism, ADHD, dyslexia, and other learning differences. Despite the growing recognition of neurodiversity, the UK schooling system has often failed to take the needs of neurodiverse students into account.

One of the most significant failures of the UK schooling system has been the lack of accommodation for students with dyslexia. Dyslexia is a learning difference that affects a person's ability to read, write, and spell. It is estimated that 10% of the UK population has dyslexia. However, many schools do not have the necessary resources or training to support students with dyslexia, leading to a significant achievement gap between neurotypical and neurodiverse students.

Another area where the UK schooling system has failed neurodiverse students is in the area of ADHD. ADHD is a condition that affects a person's ability to focus and pay attention. It is estimated that 5-7% of the UK population has ADHD. However, many schools have been slow to recognize the needs of students with ADHD, leading to a lack of accommodations and support. This can result in poor academic performance, low self-esteem, and difficulties with social relationships.

Perhaps the most egregious failure of the UK schooling system has been its treatment of autistic students. Autism is a neurological condition that affects a person's ability to communicate, socialize, and interact with others. It is estimated that 1 in 100 people in the UK are autistic. However, many schools have been woefully unprepared to accommodate the needs of autistic students, leading to significant difficulties for these students and their families.

One of the reasons why the UK schooling system has failed neurodiverse students is because of a lack of understanding and awareness of these conditions. Many educators are not trained to recognize the signs of dyslexia, ADHD, or autism, which can lead to a lack of accommodations and support. Additionally, there is a persistent stigma surrounding neurodiversity, which can make it difficult for students and their families to access the support they need.

As I write and account for myself, a Black British neurodiverse woman, I can very plainly and shortly tell you that I hated school.

Despite this Chapter being titled "I hate School" my first memories of school were quite positive. Primary school started off well for me. In Reception at the age of 4, I had a wonderful teacher called Ms Sadler who I absolutely loved. In her class, my friends and I would play with dolls and toys, it was a classroom full of fun.

However, even from this young age when Ms Sadler was teaching us, how to spell our names I really struggled with how to spell and write it. I remember thinking that this was due to the length of my name rather than any issues I may have had with spelling in general. Ms Sadler also never raised this as a problem with me or my parents as it is quite common for young children to have issues with spelling. Despite this, I have fond memories of not feeling alone as I had my best friend Teresa, and we were the only two black girls in our class.

Unfortunately, my fond memories of Reception class are where my enjoyment and love of school ended. In Year 1 Teresa moved away, and from Year 1 to the end of primary school I consistently felt traumatised, overlooked and ignored. At times I felt publicly humiliated by some of my teachers, my Year 2 teacher especially. She would draw me out in front of the whole class, command me to stand in front and answer a question and when I got it wrong, she would scold me verbally but pinch my arm physically.

This happened often and was a recurring issue, in fact, I have a vivid memory of sitting on a red carpet playing with a girl's hair whom we will call Nicky, when I should have been focusing on subtraction. However, I was trying to plat her silky blonde hair into a braid, Mrs Key noticed and called my name "Shayeta, do you know the answer?!". (For your information Shayeta is not, in fact, the correct pronunciation of my name, unfortunately, the school just never managed to get it right.)

Again, Mrs Key commanded me to come to the front and stand up in front of the whole class. She again asked me to answer the question and when I couldn't answer she started to apply pressure with her long and sharp nails and pinch my arm. This was traumatising and upsetting and made worse by the fact that when I told my parents they confronted her at parents' evening and to my dismay she straight up denied it. I couldn't help but feel like if I was a white child this situation would not have happened.

Now if it wasn't made apparent Mrs Key was an elderly Caucasian woman, who seemed to lack exposure and grace. A person who contributed to the academic failure and hopelessness I often felt at such a young age. What if circumstances were different? What if I had a teacher who understood my background and culture and could inspire me to reach for the stars? I wonder what a turn of events it would have had. These were the thoughts that plagued me as I struggled through school.

I hated all the subjects that I studied at school, and I wish I had opportunities to express myself through more art forms. Singing in assembly was the best part of the school week for me, it was the only time that I didn't have to worry about feeling different or strange. Although I was not necessarily alone, I often felt alone during primary school. I was constantly worrying about why people did not understand why I did things and acted in a certain way.

The Impact of racial inequality on Students

A 2020 report by Runnymede found that not only is the education system racially unequal in the proportion of teachers from a Black, Asian or ethnic minority background, but also that '"racism is deeply embedded in schooling". This is reflected in the views of 49% of young Black people, who thought that racism was the biggest barrier to attaining success at school.

In interviews with teachers, Runnymede found there is a shared agreement of a need for better diversity amongst teachers, providing role models for ethnic minority pupils. It is implied this would raise aspiration and thereby, their attainment. Even today, just 6% of headteachers are from an ethnic minority background. There is a risk, pupils from ethnic minority backgrounds will perceive themselves as less suited to leadership roles than their White peers. There is a need for representation to be addressed at all levels and holistically. Like Primary School, my Secondary School was also Catholic, and my parents had deliberately chosen it with the expectation that it would foster academic excellence in my sister and me. We were one of the few black students in a predominantly White school. There were only a handful of other students of colour in my year and we were still vastly outnumbered by our White peers. Despite this, thankfully there was less of a focus on my academic abilities, due to there being more children with a range of academic abilities. However, this also meant that I had to navigate academics on my own because there was less support offered. In School I wasn't a shy person, however, I was frustrated with the lack of diversity. I always dreamed of attending a school with people that looked like me and understood me.

Unlike Primary School, Secondary School wasn't as traumatic for me, but that's not to say it was an easy ride. I still faced my fair share of struggles and challenges, and often found myself feeling overwhelmed and uncertain about how to navigate this new phase of my education. While I wasn't subjected to the same level of trauma that I experienced in Primary School, the journey was far from smooth sailing. Struggling with lessons and lacking support from the staff, I found myself falling behind in school. Despite having been placed in sets based on my SATS performance, I was eventually demoted from set 3 to set 4 out of 5 in both Maths and English. It was a frustrating and demoralizing experience, and I often felt like I was floundering without the necessary resources and guidance to succeed.

At the time, my teacher showed little to no concern, not just for me, but for the entire class. It was clear that she wasn't putting in any effort to assist her students, and her lack of engagement and support was disheartening. Despite my efforts to seek her guidance and ask for advice on how I could improve, she never offered any tangible help or support, leaving me feeling frustrated and hopeless about my academic prospects.

It was a common perception among students that the teachers only showed interest and made efforts with students in the higher sets - sets 1, 2, or 3. However, looking back, I'm convinced that many of my peers in sets 4 and 5 were neurodiverse and had an attention deficit hyperactivity disorder (ADHD). The concentration levels of these students were often low, and there were frequent fights and disruptions in these classes, drawing attention away from the lesson and resulting in inadequate coverage of the curriculum.

Plagued with disappointment

As my GCSE exams approached, I dedicated myself to a rigorous revision regime that involved using various resources, including CGP books, Bitesize online, and privately funded tuition paid for by my parents. In total, I took 25 exams, and unlike previous years, we were the first cohort to sit all exams during the summer, following the linear system. I was grateful for the opportunity to sit the Triple Science exams, as it was a requirement to be pushed up to a set 2 or

1 to take the paper. Despite my desire to take on the higher exams for Maths and English, my teachers doubted my capability to pass them. Consequently, I had to settle for the foundation exam, which presented a greater challenge, with the highest attainable grade being a C.

Despite dedicating a significant amount of time to revising for my GCSEs, I was left feeling bitterly disappointed on 'results day'. It was a frustrating experience, as I truly believed that I had the potential to excel and felt disheartened that none of my efforts seemed to have paid off.

The day of my GCSE results was meant to be one of the happiest days of my life. I had poured my heart and soul into my studies, revising tirelessly for weeks and months leading up to the exams. I had even sought out additional support from tutors and educational resources to help me prepare to the best of my ability. But when I saw my results, I was plagued with disappointment and overcome with a sense of bitterness.

It was a frustrating and confusing experience. I had worked incredibly hard and believed that I had the potential to achieve excellent grades. Yet, none of my efforts seemed to have paid off, and I was left with results that were far below my expectations. I felt disheartened and defeated, wondering if all the time and effort I had invested in my studies had been in vain.

It was difficult to process that despite all my hard work, I was not able to achieve the results that I had hoped for. It felt like a crushing blow, and I struggled to come to terms with the reality of the situation. It was a painful and challenging experience, and one that left a lasting impression on me.

Despite the disappointment, however, I knew that I couldn't give up. I resolved to continue working hard and pushing myself to be the best that I could be, no matter what challenges I might face along the way.

Throughout my academic journey, I've often felt that my teachers didn't show much interest or concern in my progress. This lack of support left me feeling disheartened and demotivated, wondering if I was somehow falling short of their expectations. Over time, I began to wonder if their disinterest was linked to my race, and if I was being judged based on stereotypes and preconceptions rather than my actual abilities. This suspicion was difficult to confront, but it was impossible to ignore the nagging feeling that I wasn't being given a fair chance to succeed.

This feeling was later reinforced when having a conversation, with a colleague who was formerly a teaching assistant in a diverse area. He emphasised that from his experience there seemed to be a clear bias when it comes to testing and screening BAME (Black, Asian, and Minority Ethnic) children, particularly those who have neurodiverse conditions like dyslexia, autism, and ADHD.

According to my colleague, many teachers fail to recognise that some Black and ethnic minority children's behaviours may be attributed to neurodiversity, instead attributing them to cultural differences or simply labelling them as "naughty" children. This lack of understanding is compounded by the fact that there is often little effort made to promote cultural and religious diversity within the teaching profession.

As a result of this disconnect, I've experienced first-hand how BAME neurodiverse children often fall through the cracks, without being properly screened or given the support they need to succeed. It's a frustrating and unfair reality, and one that I believe needs to be addressed urgently if we are to create a more inclusive and equitable educational system for all students.

Data from the UK Department for Education reveals significant disparities in educational outcomes between Black children and their White British peers. In 2021, the attainment gap between disadvantaged pupils and their peers was 9.2 percentage points, but for Black pupils, the gap widened to 23.6 percentage points. This suggests that Black children are disproportionately affected by the challenges facing disadvantaged students in England. Additionally, the proportion of Black pupils achieving a grade 5 or above in English and maths GCSEs in 2019/2020 was below the national average, highlighting further disparities in educational attainment. These statistics point to systemic issues in the UK education system, which needs to be addressed to ensure equal opportunities for all students.

The Impact of Representation

As fate would have it, I found myself enrolled in a new school. This was no ordinary institution; it was a sixth form for students who didn't get the required grades to go to college. And to make matters worse, the institution had relocated to the building of one of the most notorious schools in Nottingham. A School on the other side of the city. I was filled with a sense of apprehension and uncertainty stepping into this new environment, wondering if it would be any different from my previous academic experiences.

I called it "Year 11+". The school's decision to provide me with a sixth-form experience was a generous gesture that allowed me to feel like I wasn't missing out on anything. It was a refreshing change of pace from the disappointment and frustration I had experienced in my previous academic endeavours. The opportunity to continue my education in a new environment, surrounded by peers who were also trying to make the best of a difficult situation, was a welcome change. I was determined to make the most of this second chance and prove to myself and the world what I could achieve, regardless of the setbacks I had faced.

After failing my GCSEs, I knew I had to work hard to get back on track. I redid my Maths and English GCSEs whilst taking

Level 2 BTEC courses in Creative Media and ICT. We were required to do BTEC courses to keep us busy, and I was determined to put the work in and succeed. To my surprise "Year 11+" was really when things started to really turn around for me.

My experience at this School was incredible, not only were the students diverse, but the teaching faculty was made up of teachers of colour who genuinely cared about their students' success. This was a complete game-changer for me. So in an environment where I felt seen and supported was life changing. I was able to connect with my teachers and build relationships with them, which made me more motivated to learn and grow. I felt like I finally had a community that believed in me and my potential. Looking back, I realise how important representation is in education. Seeing teachers who looked like me and shared similar experiences gave me hope and inspiration to pursue my goals.

I formed some incredible bonds with my peers during my time in school. We were a tight-knit group, and I think one of the reasons for that was that many of us were neurodiverse whether diagnosed or undiagnosed and culturally diverse. It was special to be around people who understood what I was going through and who accepted me for who I am. The support we gave each other was invaluable, and I am grateful for the friendships I made.

Throughout my academic journey, I noticed a significant improvement in my academic attainment and overall academic performance when I had teachers of colour. For me, being taught by Black, Asian, and Jewish teachers was truly revolutionary. It was the first time I had ever seen teachers that looked like me, and it was a life-changing experience.

Having teachers who shared or comprehended my cultural background allowed me to develop deep and meaningful relationships with them. I felt understood and seen in a way that I never had before in a school setting. The representation was crucial, as seeing someone who looked like me in a position of authority and knowledge made me feel like I, too, could achieve academic success.

According to a 2020 study published in the journal Social Psychological and Personality Science by researchers from the University of Georgia and North-western University, the influence of same-race teachers on Black elementary school students was investigated. The study found that Black students who had at least one Black teacher in elementary school were more likely to graduate from high school and consider attending college. The positive effects were particularly strong for Black boys from low-income families. The researchers suggest that having same-race teachers may provide students with positive role models and enhance their sense of belonging in school.

This study highlights the importance of representation in schools, particularly for students from marginalised communities. By diversifying the teaching staff, schools can create a more inclusive and supportive environment for all students.

Sadly, I also know that this kind of representation is not always possible, especially in areas with a lack of diversity in the teaching staff. Growing up, the lack of diversity among my teachers was stark. It was challenging to feel understood and supported when I couldn't connect with my teachers on a cultural level.

As a result, I strongly encourage teachers to make an intentional effort to understand diverse cultures and backgrounds. It's a crucial step in helping students who are struggling and feeling isolated. By taking the time to understand and appreciate different cultures, teachers can create a more welcoming and inclusive learning environment for all students, regardless of their race, ethnicity, or cultural background.

3

Late Diagnosis

A study by John M. Fletcher, PhD, states that Black children are 2.5 times less likely to be identified as having dyslexia than White children. According to expert Jannett Morgan, most young Black British people in the UK do not acquire a formal diagnosis until they are in university and are pushed to their limits. Unfortunately, I happen to prove this study, as this was the case for me too.

As I continued through Primary school, I was often taken out of the classroom for "special lessons". I was accompanied by 4 other students, some diagnosed with learning difficulties and other conditions. Their parents had close relationships with the teaching assistant, they seemed to be in the loop.

When it came to my parents, not only were they not aware, but they were not informed. With no phone call home or mention in a school report or parents evening. I was missing out on lessons with the rest of my classmates, learning a completely different syllabus that I would not be assessed on. We would go into a small and enclosed room learning easy exercises that I already knew. The other children would call me a genius because I already knew the answer to the questions. Despite the other student's encouragement and affirmations, I knew I was falling behind the rest of the class, I hated it. Being taken out of class came with a stigma and I felt inadequate in comparison to the rest of my class. Culturally I already felt like there was an invisible barrier.

My best friend at the time also attended the special lessons, thinking back I'm pretty sure she was neurodiverse too, I felt like we could understand each other. However, at one point they started letting her stay in the classroom because her Mum called the school to complain. I didn't tell my parents, they had no clue what was going on, all of this made me feel even more isolated. Looking back now, I wish I had told my parents.

Throughout Primary, it became clear that the school knew that there was an issue regarding my learning. In fact, when I took my year 6 SATs exams, I was given a reader to assist me. The reader was warm and lovely, encouraging, and helpful. Motivating and reassuring, telling me that I already knew the answers. She was the Grandmother of one of my classmates, and "Diane" seemed to be exposed. My race and culture did not seem like a barrier for her.

Unbelievably, I scored highly in my SATs Exams, and this was largely down to having a reader. I was put in mid to top-ranking sets in Secondary school but was swiftly moved down. I did not have any support and struggled to concentrate in my lessons. Even then, no teacher flagged any issues with this. There were no questions about why I may have moved down sets so quickly. To be honest, most of the teachers at my secondary school did not seem interested.

I was not screened for Dyslexia. Quite frankly I did not know anyone else who was screened for any condition there. The children with a diagnosis were screened and diagnosed before they even came to Secondary School. These children were given extra time and support and I remember a girl in my class who had a special Laptop and magnifying glass to read. Things that I too in my later years of study would also acquire.

It was not until year 11+ that I first received a computer-based Dyslexia screening. Despite the difficulties that I had at school, I did not think that I was Dyslexic. I had always found ways to work around things that did not work for me. Whilst it was not always easy, I was a confident reader and writer. Not the quickest writer, however, my vocabulary and articulation were beyond my years.

Although I had always soldiered on to get there, from wobbly pages, stutters and stammers, an exponential difference, and a completely different person. From countless hours of tuition and many failed tests, each experience deposited another level of determination and grit. So, to me, it was a surprise that the Dyslexia screening results came back inconclusive.

I didn't know how to feel, it was not necessarily a confirmation, however, it did create room for doubt. Regardless, I did not want to fixate on what could or could not be. Whilst the screening test was designed to give me an indication of possible dyslexic difficulties, it was not an official diagnosis. However, it was a starting point.

According to a 2019 survey by the British Dyslexia Association, 80% of schools in the UK offer some form of dyslexia screening. Unfortunately for me both my Primary and Secondary school fell between the 20% that didn't. Something I'd like to advocate for is to make testing more readily available within Schools. Whilst a diagnosis can only be made by a qualified professional, a screening test is a starting point. It's a dream of mine for every child within the UK educational system to be offered a free dyslexia screening. It's important for children to know that there are options out there when required. Early screening tests would enable children to receive more insight and understanding into how they may learn. Enabling them to start the journey to receiving the support and adjustments that they are entitled to sooner. Overall, giving them the opportunity to perform to their highest output with confidence and assurance.

4

Light at the end of the Tunnel

This chapter is titled Light at the End of the Tunnel, but it does not initially start off that way... Believe it or not, I failed my GCSE's, again. A good three months after year 11 GCSE results day, I re-took my Maths and English exams and to my dismay, I had failed them both, yet again.

Heart-breaking, I was adamant to acquire a grade C. I was desperate to progress onto the next level and needed to attend a real sixth form to begin. With AS-Level and A-Levels, I could be accepted into university, a goal for many African and Caribbean children. An achievement gloried and put on a pedestal by our community. Enabling one to fulfil the African Caribbean dream, or should I say the African Caribbean parent's dream? The Role of African and Caribbean Parents in Their Children's Educational Aspirations Journal by Karen A. Johnson states "African and Caribbean parents have always wanted their children to be doctors, lawyers, and engineers." However, what happens when you can't or don't meet these standards, requirements or expectations?

For me, I wanted to attend university, but not to study Law, Medicine or Engineering. I wanted to study Fashion Marketing. I had always considered myself a creative rather than an Academic. University to me symbolised financial independence and physical freedom. For many African children, going to university is often liberation from their parents' strict and rigid regime. Something that for many African and Caribbean parents can come from the pressures and struggles of being a first-generation immigrant. With many requirements and tight leashes wrapped around their children in the need for them to justify their journey.

A peculiar case, fortunately for me my parents were on the softer side, particularly when it came to matters concerning me. During this time, my parents did their best to support me, providing me with private tuition for Maths and English, alongside encouraging and affirming me. They didn't seem too concerned about the profession or the course that I would study. My mother's only prerogative was that I attend university, and my father's was that I follow through to higher education, no matter the facet it manifested in.

When it came to studying, I did my part, working hard and doing my best. After my second attempt of trying to acquire my GCSEs, I started to speculate why I was failing. Was there something bigger at play? Potentially I had learning difficulties or maybe I was cursed. Learning difficulties may have been the most rational thought, however, I opted for being cursed. I chose to intensify my prayers, alongside increasing my involvement within the church.

My church at the time was God sent, it was multicultural and multigenerational and I started attending off the back of a youth group. Every week I was confronted with an affirming message of faith and always left feeling uplifted and encouraged.

I pencilled in my next opportunity, June 2014, the next time I could re-sit. I dedicated all my effort, energy, and prayers to acquiring my GCSE Maths and English. I had a plan, and I was certain that I would catch up with the rest of my peers. I was determined that I was not going to be left behind.

Finally, after 3 attempts, in the summer of 2014, my prayers were answered. I had acquired a Grade C GCSE Qualification in both Maths and English. Although it was just a pass mark I was over the moon, it enabled me to successfully enrol and start Level 3 and AS courses. It meant that I was one step closer to my plan.

That year, my faith had increased, and I was certain that I would go to university a year earlier than expected. As they say, "Faith without works is dead." So, I sacrificed £22 of my pocket money and paid a year earlier for UCAS, the UK Universities and Colleges Admissions Service. Although I had no guarantee of being accepted, I spent time writing my personal statement and collecting references. I sent applications to Manchester Metropolitan University, The

University of Manchester, Nottingham Trent University and Keele University.

Out of four of the universities two offers were received many of them with the condition to earn 240-280 UCAS points. Unbelievably, after my first year of sixth form alone, I was expected to acquire enough UCAS points to enter university, not necessarily a Russel Group university, but a university atlas.

Now things do not always go to plan, my expectations that I had to acquire 240 UCAS points on results day, went down the drain. Unfortunately, when it came to my AS Religious Studies and Photography my points were acquitted to 40 credits. However, due to acquiring Distinction stars in Level 3 Business studies, I received a very generous 120 UCAS points. Giving me a collective total of 160 points. Not as high as I anticipated, but potentially enough credits to get into university via clearing.

After receiving my results, I called Nottingham Trent University University's clearing line and to my dismay, they informed me that I did not have enough UCAS points. Faith-filled and believing that I was going to university that year I called them again, and a different person answered the phone but gave me the same answer. So, I called and considered another nearby University, De Mont Fort. I called them, and they offered me a place through clearing. However, when I disclosed that I had not yet sat my A-Levels they revoked their offer.

I was disappointed, however, I never lost faith and I took a quick minute to pray. In that moment I received an epiphany from a conversation that had occurred with a friend in the year above. In this conversation, they mentioned that they were applying to the University of Lincoln.

Although unfamiliar, I called them to enquire about a space, to my surprise, I was offered a space and I was invited to enrol in person. This is what I had prayed for, however, I was in disbelief and hesitant to proceed. I had never heard of anyone who went to university after just 1 year of A-levels. My teachers were also full of disbelief and my mother was full of joy. The decision was down to me, and I decided to attend enrolment. I submitted the required documents, and it was official I was a University of Lincoln Student.

To God be the glory, not only did this give me the opportunity to Graduate, but it gave me the space and the means to start my own business. This enabled me to utilise my connections and student finance to start my first Business, a faith-based clothing brand called Trend Savvy.

I was graced with the opportunity to pursue further testing and screening for dyslexia, and I was referred to a qualified educational psychologist with £500+ expenses covered by the Disability Student Allowance. Something that I was able to pursue due to the prompting from my mother to enquire and pursue an official diagnosis from my University's wellbeing centre.

5

My Diagnosis

With just a two-week wait and I was able to acquire an in-person appointment. Although it was my second Dyslexia screening, it was the first time that I had ever had one in person. When I got to the University Wellbeing Centre, I was greeted by a learning support advisor and asked a selection of questions linked to my learning. It was nice to be able to talk to someone about my fears and struggles. For the first time, I finally felt heard.

The results came back straight away, indicating that I would need to be referred to an educational psychologist. Whilst this was processed and scheduled, I waited a few months. Again, I had no other option but to solider through and navigate much of my learning alone during my first year of university.

Finally, the day had come, my dyslexia examination was here. It was my first time meeting an educational psychologist and the exam was extensive. The examination took over 2 hours and ranged from writing tests to reading tests and to my surprise a pattern and shapes test. After the examination I was exhausted, it felt like I had mentally run a marathon. Now I just had to wait for the results.

The results took a couple of months to come, it was not until the beginning of my second year that I received my diagnosis. I was Dyslexic, and not only was I Dyslexic I was Dyscalculic and Dyspraxic.

I was overwhelmed with joy and sadness, and I cried. Before this diagnosis, there were many years of doubt, and this report and diagnosis addressed all of them. [A brief overview of the report can be found below.]

Background Information

A request was made for a psychological assessment for Oluseyitan to ascertain whether she has a specific learning difficulty and to help process any needs relating to course and examination access arrangements as well as consideration for DSA (Disabled Students Allowance). I assessed Oluseyitan on 14th December 2016 at Dyslexia Action in Lincoln. The present report describes the procedure and the results of the assessment undertaken by Oluseyitan.

Oluseyitan reported that she is in the first year of a three-year BA (Hons) in Marketing at the University of Lincoln. She reported difficulties with written work (speed, essay structure, coherence, getting her ideas onto paper, note-taking and proof-reading) and reading (reading aloud, speed and needing to reread text to take it in). She explained that she used to have difficulties with spelling and handwriting but had tutor support. Oluseyitan also reported difficulties with short-term memory, organisation, time management/meeting deadlines, attention/concentration and balance-ordination. She also reported difficulties with aspects of maths (finances, algebra, equations, times tables, angles). She explained that she gained her GCSE Maths (grade C) on a second attempt.

On her questionnaire, Oluseyitan reported difficulties around aspects of communication, organisation, memory and concentration, literacy, orientation, arithmetic and co-ordination/ dexterity. She reported no symptoms of visual stress/Irlen Syndrome.

Oluseyitan also completed the Adult Developmental Co-ordination Disorder/Dyspraxia Checklist (ADC) for Further and Higher Education. Oluseyitan reported frequent difficulties as a child with self-care tasks, learning to ride a bike, team games, writing neatly and at speed, playing a musical instrument and organisation. She reported current frequent difficulties with eating with a knife/fork/spoon, hobbies requiring good co-ordination, writing neatly and at speed, copying down information, organisation, finding her way around new places, sitting still, losing things, learning to drive, team sports, dancing and multi-tasking. An analysis of her questionnaire suggests that she is at risk of developmental co-ordination disorder/ dyspraxia.

Oluseyitan left school at 18 years of age. She reported a history of difficulties through school (reading, spelling, handwriting, maths, essays, revision, sports and games) and had Teaching Assistant support from Y2-Y6 (for literacy and numeracy), as well as a tutor for maths in Y6-12. She reported that she had a reader for SAT's in Y6. There is a possible family history of specific learning difficulties. Oluseyitan reported no difficulties with vision (with glasses) or hearing. She reported no serious illnesses/injuries or side effects from medication that might impact on today's assessment.

Test Conditions

Oluseyitan presented as a motivated individual who worked diligently across a wide range of assessment activities and concentrated well throughout. She reported feeling well on the day of her assessment. No special test conditions were required.

Other Diagnostic Assessment

Oluseyitan was asked to complete the York Spoonerism Test'. This test is designed to assess whether a person can segment single-syllable words and then synthesise the segments to provide new words or word combinations. This test taps into phonological awareness of speech sounds within words), a key factor in the development of literacy and often an area of weakness for people with dyslexia. Oluseyitan scored in the average range 40th percentile) for accuracy but below average (5th - 15th percentile) for speed.

Oluseyitan also completed the Beery VMI test. This examines an individual's ability to integrate or Co-ordinate their visual-perceptual and motor (finger and hand movement) abilities. Research has shown that individuals with developmental coordination disorder/dyspraxia perform less well on the Beery VMI than their peers. Oluseyitan scored in the below-average range (3rd percentile) in her age range.

Oluseyitan was also asked to complete the Rapid Digit Naming subtest of the Comprehensive Test of Phonological Processing (2nd Edition) - CTOPP-2. This requires individuals to rapidly name rows of numbers on a page. Her score was in the average range (25th percentile).

Oluseyitan was also asked to complete the Rapid Letter Naming subtest of the CTOPP-2. This requires individuals to rapidly name rows of letters on a page. Her score was in the well below average (1st percentile).

Conclusion

During today's assessment, Oluseyitan's overall level of ability lay in the below average range in her age range. However, her cognitive profile was irregular. Relative strengths were observed in Oluseyitan's verbal reasoning skills. Weaknesses were observed in her non- verbal reasoning skills, ability to process visual information at speed and auditory working memory.

Oluseyitan's word reading skills were below the level expected in relation to her age and verbal reasoning skills. Her reading comprehension, spelling and numerical operations skills were at the level expected in relation to her age, although below the level expected in relation to her verbal reasoning skills. Oluseyitan read at a below average pace on a test of reading efficiency and demonstrated some difficulties with accuracy when reading non-words. She wrote at an average pace on a free writing task and at a low average pace on a copying task. Oluseyitan's handwriting was legible. She demonstrated mild difficulties with spelling and sentence structure/coherence. Oluseyitan's graphic writing speed was below average, and her error rate was 50%. Oluseyitan demonstrated difficulties with phonological processing (processing of the sounds in words) at speed, although no difficulties with accuracy. She demonstrated difficulties with perceptual-visual/motor integration.

"Taking everything into consideration, I am of the opinion that Oluseyitan does have dyspraxia, as well as mild dyslexia and dyscalculia". It was a journey to navigate and understand what these conditions meant and for the longest time, I found myself googling definitions and relating them to myself and circumstances.

Dyspraxia - a common disorder that affects movement and coordination. Dyspraxia does not affect your intelligence. It can affect your coordination skills - such as tasks requiring balance, playing sports, or learning to drive a car.

Dyslexia - a common learning difficulty that mainly causes problems with reading, writing, and spelling. It's a specific learning difficulty, which means it causes problems with certain abilities used for learning, such as reading and writing. Intelligence isn't affected.

Dyscalculia - a specific and persistent difficulty in understanding numbers which can lead to a diverse range of difficulties with mathematics.

Autism is still a condition that I have not yet been tested for. The NHS Common signs of autism in adults, such as "taking things very literally – for example, you may not understand sarcasm or phrases like "break a leg" and "finding it hard to understand what others are thinking or feeling". Signs that very much resonate with me, however, a full evaluation has been a deterrent due to the high cost. According to The Royal College of Psychiatrists, the cost of an autism assessment in the UK can range from £250 to £1,500. For many like me this is a very high cost, and although the NHS may offer these services many are confronted with the challenge of long lists and wait times.

ADHD is another condition that I have not yet been extensively tested for. ADHD is an abbreviation for attention deficit hyperactivity disorder. The symptoms of attention deficit hyperactivity disorder (ADHD) can be categorised into 2 types, inattentiveness (difficulty concentrating and focusing) and hyperactivity and impulsiveness.

The NHS Common signs of hyperactivity and impulsiveness are "being unable to sit still, especially in calm or quiet surroundings", "constantly fidgeting", "being unable to concentrate on tasks", "excessive physical movement" and "excessive talking". The NHS Common signs of Inattentiveness (difficulty concentrating and focusing) are "having a short attention span and being easily distracted", "making careless mistakes – for example, in schoolwork", "appearing forgetful or losing things" and "constantly changing activity or task". According to the ADHD Foundation the cost of an ADHD assessment can range from £200 to £1,000. Again, for many like me this is a very high cost, and although the NHS may offer these services many are confronted with the challenge of long lists and wait times. According to the NHS ADHD Waiting Time Survey by ADHD Action the waiting time for an assessment in some cases can be up to 18 months.

6

Lack of funding

Attending a small Catholic school as a neurodiverse individual was a challenge. Both Primary and Secondary Schools I attended received limited amounts of state funding, lacking the resources required to offer adequate neurodiversity screening and testing.

It said that funding is allocated based on the number of pupils and the school's level of need. For many Catholic Schools, in comparison to mainstream schools, it seems that funding tends to be limited. This may be due to a smaller number of students within some of these schools, resulting in some schools receiving less funding.

Despite this, both faith-based and faithless schools have been affected by government budget cuts. And in 2019, a report by the National Education Union found that funding cuts had led to a reduction in the number of teaching assistants, support staff, and pastoral care in schools. With a potential negative impact on children with special educational needs. The report found that Catholic schools were among the worst affected by the funding cuts.

A 2019 survey by the British Dyslexia Association found that 65% of schools in England, 62% of schools in Wales, and 60% of schools in Scotland reported having conducted a dyslexia assessment in the previous year. However, I don't remember getting tested for Dyslexia, Dyscalculia or Dyspraxia at school. In fact, no records or documents can be found. Perhaps for my school, these tests were not conducted due to a lack of state funding. I acknowledge that whilst screening may be free testing is not and this may be a deterrent/ difficulty for many schools. However, this was not the case for one of my friends who happened to attend a private school, she was able to receive a Dyslexia test within the confounds of her school. Potentially this was due to the school having access to more funding and as a result better resources to support their students. I always wonder what extra support and adjustments I would have received at Secondary School, if only I was tested and diagnosed sooner.

According to the British Dyslexia Association in the United Kingdom, the cost of a dyslexia assessment can range from £250 to £1,500. When I conducted my test at university the cost was over £500, fortunately for me, due to this being conducted during my studies my test was covered by

Disabled Students' Allowance. This is a Godsend, as for many students do not necessarily have £500 of disposable income to spare for a Dyslexia examination.

Although not affluent, my parents always found a way to support my educational needs. They invested in private tutors, revision books, and anything I asked for in relation to my studies. I acknowledge how fortunate I was to have parents who believed in me and were willing to invest in my education. They were persistent and resilient and even provided me with a Supplementary School, also known as "Saturday School".

Shiefton Supplementary School provided supplementary education in Mathematics, English and African Studies. It was created to address the concern of parents who did not wish to have their child/children underachieve in mainstream schools. We met every Saturday during term time between 9.30 am and 12.30 pm. Students came from predominantly Caribbean/ African descent and an active parent group met regularly to discuss matters relating to the curriculum and the running of the school. And although I did not appreciate it at the time, I am now immensely grateful for the contribution that Shiefton had on my life. Especially when came to representation and the opportunity to learn African Studies, something that I was not given in my mainstream School. Unfortunately, Shiefton is no longer running today, however, I will always honour its impact.

Despite the deficit I felt I received from my state school education, I eventually excelled and flourished academically, achieving a Bachelor of Honours and Master of Arts degree, with Distinction. But I still question what if I was tested sooner. Would I have endured all that I endured?

With the knock to my confidence and all those failed tests, I would hate for someone else to go through what I went through. And so, my dream is for screening and testing to be made more readily available within state schools, to advocate for more people to pursue testing and to reduce the stigma of neurodiversity within black communities.

As mentioned previously, whilst a diagnosis can only be made by a qualified professional, a screening test is a starting point. It's a dream of mine for every child within the UK educational system to be boldly offered a free dyslexia screening at every point of their educational journey. It is important for children to know that there are options out there when required. Early screening tests would enable children to receive more insight and understanding into how they may learn. Enabling them to start the journey to receiving the support and adjustments that they are entitled to sooner. Overall, giving them the opportunity to perform to their highest output, with confidence and assurance.

7

My Superpower

With everything that I have experienced, today I can acknowledge and testify that Neurodiversity is indeed my Superpower. Conditions that were once seen as obstacles and limitations have since become the catalysts for my greatest strength. Shaping my perception and outlook on the world, attributing to my creativity and boldness. Making me resilient in the face of adversity and challenges. Join me as I share the profound lessons I have learned from my conditions, unveiling the remarkable superpowers that lie within.

Lesson 1: Adaptability

I have always embraced change and unleashed my creativity. Dyspraxia has taught me the power of adaptability. Rather than succumbing to frustration and giving up, I have learned to embrace change and thrive in ever-shifting environments. This adaptability has become my superpower, enabling me to tackle problems from unconventional angles and think outside the box. It has unleashed a wellspring of creativity within me, allowing me to innovate, create, and express myself in unique and awe-inspiring ways. I have discovered that adaptability is not a weakness but a remarkable strength that sets me apart.

The Developmental Medicine and Child Neurology study was published in 2007. The study involved 150 children with dyspraxia and 150 children without dyspraxia. The children were given a number of tests to assess their creativity, including tests of drawing, story-telling, and problem-solving. The study found that the children with dyspraxia scored significantly higher on the creativity tests than the children without dyspraxia. I particularly saw this adaptability and creativity when it came to my master's degree. I was faced with my final project and instead of writing a traditional dissertation, I chose to lean into my strengths and produce a 30-minute documentary, that was later awarded a Distinction.

Lesson 2: Multidimensional Thinking

 My story alone testifies that I have transcended boundaries and embraced creative brilliance. Dyslexia has gifted me with the ability to think multi-dimensionally. Instead of seeing it as a reading and writing difficulty, I have learned to harness this superpower. My mind effortlessly visualises complex concepts and patterns, enabling me to approach problems holistically and make connections that others may overlook. This multidimensional thinking has propelled me to push boundaries, shatter limitations, and embark on creative endeavours that have left an indelible mark on the world. Dyslexia has taught me that my mind is a wellspring of creative brilliance, and that I can achieve extraordinary things.

According to the Journal of the Scientific American Mind, there is often a need for people with dyslexia to find creative ways to solve problems that come up in their everyday lives. This can lead to a strong ability to think outside the box and come up with innovative solutions. For example, Walt Disney, who was dyslexic, was able to use his problem-solving skills to create some of the most iconic animated films of all time. For myself, thinking out of the box and outside the traditional educational system links to this. Particularly in the instance of obtaining admission to a university with just one year of AS-Levels.

Lesson 3: The Forge of Tenacity and Strategic Mastery

Close your eyes and imagine a world where numbers appear as complex riddles waiting to be unravelled. That's the realm of dyscalculia, my constant companion. Despite my struggles with mathematics, I have discovered an extraordinary superpower within—tenacity and unwavering work ethic. Each numerical challenge I encounter becomes a stepping-stone for growth and self-improvement. With an unyielding spirit, I confront these obstacles head-on, drawing upon my strategic brilliance to find innovative solutions. Rest assured, my journey proves that even in the face of math-related difficulties, determination and hard work can guide us to remarkable achievements.

According to The National-Centre for Learning Disabilities, The National Centre for Learning Disabilities estimates that 3-7% of the population has dyscalculia. For something so uncommon there is a Forge of Tenacity and Strategic Mastery that can come. A trait that is displayed and present in all that I do. No matter the size of the difficulty, whether big or small I never give up. Today, there are many challenges that I face trying to navigate a neurotypical world, however, I have vowed to myself to never give up.

In conclusion, my journey has led me to embrace neurodiversity as my superpower. What was once seen as obstacles and limitations have become catalysts for my greatest strengths. Dyspraxia has taught me adaptability, allowing me to thrive in ever-shifting environments and think outside the box, unleashing my creativity. Dyslexia has gifted me with multidimensional thinking, enabling me to approach problems holistically and make unique connections. Dyscalculia has forged my tenacity and strategic mastery, pushing me to overcome challenges and achieve remarkable feats.

Research has shown that individuals with dyspraxia exhibit higher creativity scores, highlighting the power of adaptability and thinking differently. Similarly, people with dyslexia often find innovative solutions and think outside the box, as exemplified by notable figures like Walt Disney. Dyscalculia, although less common, has been shown to foster determination and a strong work ethic.

Despite the difficulties I face in a neurotypical world, I remain resilient and committed to never giving up. These lessons and experiences have shaped my perception and outlook on the world, attributing to my creativity, boldness, and unwavering spirit. By sharing my profound lessons, I aim to unveil the remarkable superpowers that lie within neurodiversity, encouraging others to embrace their unique strengths and redefine what is possible. Together, let us celebrate the beauty and potential of neurodiversity, transforming what were once perceived as limitations into extraordinary abilities.

Printed in Great Britain
by Amazon